Organize Yourself!

Organize Yourself!

A Mother/Daughter Guide to
Getting and Staying Organized
in All Aspects Of Your Life …
So You Can Have Fun!

Robin Lee Venturelli
London Alexandra Venturelli

iUniverse, Inc.
New York   Lincoln   Shanghai

Organize Yourself!
A Mother/Daughter Guide to Getting and Staying Organized in All Aspects Of Your Life … So You Can Have Fun!

iUniverse books may be ordered through booksellers or by contacting:

iUniverse
2021 Pine Lake Road, Suite 100
Lincoln, NE 68512
www.iuniverse.com
1-800-Authors (1-800-288-4677)

Because of the dynamic nature of the Internet, any Web addresses or links contained in this book may have changed since publication and may no longer be valid.

The views expressed in this work are solely those of the author and do not necessarily reflect the views of the publisher, and the publisher hereby disclaims any responsibility for them.

ISBN: 978-0-595-45072-5 (pbk)
ISBN: 978-0-595-89383-6 (ebk)

Printed in the United States of America

CONTENTS

INTRODUCTION

Organization is a concept that we all need to successfully function in the twenty-first century. There are many books and guides written to help one become better organized; Amazon.com has more than 192,000 listed under the topic. This book is a unique perspective; one arrived at through different paths, yet with one common goal, within the same household.

Half the suggestions come from a mother's perspective. Robin Venturelli was born organized. As a young child, she delighted in organizing her crayon box into rainbow order. She was wowed by the invention of carbon paper to reduce work time and make multiple copies. She became the family photographer and historian, and kept detailed records of family members dating back to the Declaration of Independence.

A life of excellent school grades, accolades from her teachers, and a graduate school grade point average of 4.3 lead to Robin's career as a public elementary school teacher. Her first year of teaching brought the award of Orange County Student Teacher of The Year from the Orange County Social Science Association. Her students became part of "Team V," and learned how to organize the various aspects of their daily lives. Robin was able to find organizational solutions for all kinds of students; ones who were born organizers and ones who were diagnosed with ADHD and had trouble staying focused. At the request of the principal, Robin taught a seminar for parents entitled, "How to Promote a Successful Home Environment."

After many successful years of teaching, Robin left the field of education to be a stay-at-home-mom, and part-time portrait photographer. She couldn't stay out of the educational environment for long, as she quickly began volunteering at her children's school. Even there, she organized her fellow moms and ended up as Chairman of the Parents Association, and a member of the Board of Trustees. Having completed her volunteer activities at school, she joined together with her seventeen year old daughter, London, to co-author this book.

London Venturelli brings teenage wisdom to her organizational skills. She doesn't have any use for a clean and tidy bedroom. Her desk is filled with piles, and she prefers to work on the floor. A second closet was added to her room to accommodate her ever-growing collection of clothes. From the time she started pre-school, she has wanted to be in charge and use her own unique style of organization, and she has proven to be quite successful at it. She knows where everything in her room is located, and in which piles her needed paperwork can be found. She has many half-filled purses, but always manages to have everything she needs when asked. She has completed her homework and studied for tests completely on her own since kindergarten. Throughout her twelve years of schooling, she organized multiple ways to balance her after-school activities, of which there were many, and her school assignments, as well as her free time. Her junior year in high school provided a challenge as she began driving, attending late night parties, studying for her first Advanced Placement exam and the S.A.T., and began to look at perspective colleges. She still, however, managed to throw a party at home for one-hundred and twenty-five classmates, make the academic Dean's List, and co-run the Student Life Center at her school. With eleventh grade behind her, she decided to help other teens cope by writing this book in conjunction with her mother.

Although reached through quite different paths, Robin and London have a common goal at the end of their organizing. They both like to organize their lives so that they can have time for additional fun. They both realized that the more they used their organization systems, the more time they had left over to do the things they truly love. Their ideas vary in strategic style; Robin is a born organizer and London is a creative organizer. No matter which category you find yourself in, their ideas are sure to bring about solutions for your organizational puzzles. Through sharing their thoughts and strategies with you, they hope that you will also enjoy your extra time to have fun.

CHAPTER I

WHERE DO I BEGIN?

If you're anything like us, your life is busy with paperwork, phone calls, email, "snail" mail, chores, social events, friends, etc … The trick to having fun in life is organizing yourself so you can enjoy life's journey. Organization provides more freedom for you to live in the moment, relax, and trust that "things are under control." In other words, you can have fun!

Some people are "born organizers." These are the types of kids who line up their clothes according to color and keep their bedroom looking like a picture postcard from an interior design store. Mom's one of these. Other people (most of us) seem to acquire organizational skills as we go through life. We learn them from teachers, friends, parents, books, and trial and error. Some of the skills seem to stick with us, while others are fleeting moments performed with good intentions that fall far short of their goal. Organization is easy if you adapt it to your individual lifestyle. London has developed unusual and creative ways to organize her life "doing it her way."

We've laid out a simple plan to get you started and keep you organized, so you can have fun. To begin using this book, take the Organizational Assessment exercise and then simply skip ahead to the chapters that reflect your needed skills. The chapters are purposely short and to-the-point, as neither of us wanted to waste any of your time with unnecessary explanations. As you begin to feel more organized, you may just find that you have the free time to read our "bonus words of wisdom chapters."

Organizational Assessment:
To begin with, think about your average day. When do you feel stressed and out of time? When do you feel relaxed and comfortable? Chances are that you need some new organization skills during your stressful time more than during your relaxation time. Begin by jotting down your typical day (feel free to make two

lists, one for weekdays and one for weekends). Next to each item, add an "s" for stressed and an "r" for relaxed. Here are our lists:

Mom:
Weekday
Make breakfast for family-s
Drive kids to school-s
Exercise-r
Get dressed-r
Chores, Cleaning, Appointments-r
Work-s and r
After School Pick Up and Kid's Activities-r
Make dinner-r
Leisure activities-r
Sleep-r

London:
Weekday
Get dressed-r
Eat breakfast-r
Drive to school-s
Attend school-s
After-School activities-r
Eat dinner-r
Do chores-s
Do Homework-s
Sleep-r

Weekend
Eat breakfast-r
Plans with friends or family-r
Catch up on paperwork or homework-s
Sleep-r

If you have all "r's, then please pass our book onto someone else who needs it more than you do. If you have any "s" times, then that is the place to begin. Go back to the table of contents page and select the chapters that best correspond with your times of stress, and begin getting organized.

CHAPTER 2

YOUR DESK

Your desk is a mini-reflection of your mind. Is it clutter free? Of course not; no ones is. The key is to organize your clutter so you can take care of business and get things accomplished. Robin's desk is spotless and London's desk is full of piles, yet both of us are completely organized. The key is finding a desk system that works for you, and one that will be functional year after year.

What style of desk-worker are you?

- Do you have your own desk? If not, it is time to set one up now. (Even a table or a nightstand can act as a desk.)

- Do you like to create piles? If so, what makes up each pile? Can those piles be put into labeled files or boxes?

- Do you like to hide things in "junk" drawers? Make it a point to clean out your junk drawers on the first of each month. Junk drawers can turn into astrological black holes before you realize it.

- Do you lack supplies? Need a stapler and can't find one? Organize a supply caddy and label your stuff. Mom likes to use a label-maker so all of her labels look alike. Conversely, I like to creatively label my notebooks and desk items with markers, magazine designs, or photos.

- Do you have a crowded desk due to mementos? Add a shelf on the wall near your desk and place all non-essential items on the shelf. Increase the number of shelves needed until you have placed all of your "cherished items" in their proper places. Once an item no longer holds the sentimental value that it once did (corsage from that junior high dance) then it's time to toss it or store it. We've both found that taking a photo of a trophy, then tossing out the item, is a great way to save the memory, but throw out the "junk."

Start by creating your own desk-type work area with a phone, computer, writing area, and file cabinet. If you don't have a home-office available, put your desk in the kitchen or in your bedroom. Pick an area where you can concentrate for at least an hour without interruptions. Use drawers and boxes instead of piles. Drawers can be labeled (files, writing utensils, stationery, bills.) See suggested file list ideas on the next page.

My husband and I have in and out boxes to pass notes and bills to each other. We avoid discussing controversial issues by jotting down a quick note to each other, and placing it in the box. For example, "Honey, how much money do you think we should spend on your father for his birthday? Do you have any ideas on what he would like? Do you want to shop for his gift or would you like us to go together? Please reply by Friday."

Make a To Do List once each week and cross off items as you accomplish them. At the end of the week, throw the old list away and start a new one. Robin prefers to keep her list on the computer, while London uses a dry-erase board in her bathroom. Robin's list is organized into priority order, with the highest priority activities at the top. London's list is organized by type of activity; things to buy, things to do, wish-list of future activities.

A Mom's Sample Household File List

o   To Be Filed (This should be emptied each month)
o   Automobile loans, documents, auto-repair receipts
o   Bank account statements
o   Cash receipts
o   Charity donations
o   Computer software information, passwords, and warrantees
o   Credit card receipts (Can be broken down into types of cards or expenses)
o   Medical receipts and insurance forms
o   School papers (Keep a separate folder for each child in the family)
o   Vacation plans/tickets (Keep in chronological order)

A Teenager's Sample Desk File List

o   File folder for each subject in school
o   Bank account statements

o   Computer Software information, passwords, and warrantees

o   Misc. school junk (If this gets too large, divide the file into smaller sub-sections)

1. Never run out of supplies. Keep two extras of everything (printer ink cartridges, rolls of stamps, boxes of paper and envelopes, pens, stationery notes, etc) in a cabinet. When you use one of your extras, immediately place the empty carton in a "replenishment box." Then, once or twice a month purchase and replace all the needed supplies that are in your box.

2. Keep at least twenty birthday/anniversary/get well/cards in a box. Include a few blank cards that can be used for any occasion. It is a waste of time to go to the store every time you need to purchase a card. If you want the card to be very specific (Happy 40th Birthday, Happy Bar Mitzvah, etc..) look at your calendar one month ahead of time, and purchase at one time all of the special cards needed for that month.

3. Keep a calendar on the wall by your desk. Make sure each date has enough space to jot down any pertinent information you want to include. I like to jot down birthdays, anniversaries and vacation dates. (Family Calendar will keep your birthdates, anniversary dates, and any other special dates on file, and reproduce them every year in a new calendar for you. 1-800-326-1225) London prefers to use Outlook Calendar on her computer.

4. The computer is your friend. Learn to use it. Order items on line instead of running errands around town. Keep a small post-it on your desk with your credit card number and website passwords.

5. Schedule time in your weekly calendar to do desk-work, or create a standing work time each day/week. When you are working at your desk, do not answer the phone. Instead, reserve time at the end of your work period to check your phone messages and return calls. If your phone company offers "Caller ID", get it so you can glance at who is calling while you continue to work. Note: When leaving a phone message on someone else's line, speak slowly and clearly. Always leave your whole message; don't just say, "Call me back." This wastes time, both yours and theirs. Always leave your phone number, even if it's a close friend. Some of London's friends find that they have to turn off their Instant Messages when they are trying to work.

6. Open your mail daily, pay bills weekly. Keep bills in a "To Be Paid" file and a "Paid Bills" file.

7. When attending a social event, do what Princess Diana did. Address and stamp a thank you note prior to attending the event. Keep the unwritten note by your bed. When you return home from the event, quickly jot down your thank you, and go to bed. Mail the note in the morning. Formal etiquette states that you have five days to write a thank you note after receiving a gift or attending an event. If the invitation was sent via email, you may email your thank you as well. Your thank you note should include the following:

   - An opening comment about your personal relationship with the recipient, i.e. "I treasure our friendship."

   - A thank you for the item you received or the event you attended.

   - A mention of how you plan to use the gift or a detail you particularly liked at the event, i.e. "I plan to use the new purse for my graduation party and all summer long." "The pasta you prepared was divine, and I found myself running back to the buffet for seconds!"

   - A final remark expressing your appreciation or good wishes for the recipient, i.e., "You are so thoughtful to remember me on my birthday."

8. Keep a bulletin board on the wall by your desk. Attach party invitations, concert, sports and theatre tickets, kid's activity schedules, and anything else you need to refer to. Keep in mind, if you are covering up one item with another, your bulletin board is either too small or too cluttered. Replace it, or weed it out.

9. Use the computer to make a list of your friend's addresses and phone numbers. Then print several copies of this list and place one copy in each car, phone, and suitcase. If you don't have an electronic PDA with an address book, you may want to add a copy to your purse.

Notes Just for Teens:

1. Keep an assignment book or electronic calendar with you at all times to write down daily homework and long-term projects. Highlight the quizzes, tests, and projects on the day they are due.

2. Keep your computer files organized (by school year, by subject, and by title.) Save and Backup all the time, or when each song ends on your stereo.

3. If you are lucky enough to have a cell phone, save the numbers on your sim card, so they will still be there when you get a new phone.

4. See chapter five on "Your Homework, Locker, & Free time"

CHAPTER 3

YOUR CLOSET

Your closet is your private domain and can be a charming place to peruse with creativity, or a den of chaos. The difference is in the organization. A well-organized closet allows you to select outfits that coordinate, to match shoes and handbags, and to wear clothes that fit, are in style, and are flattering. Being able to easily pick out your clothes each day saves you more time for fun. To tackle the closet, one needs only the motivation to begin.

The biggest job is the first one. Set aside an hour one weekend and try on your clothes. Give away anything that is permanently stained, too small, out of style, terribly uncomfortable, or has "bad karma." Enlist the help of a friend, or possibly your mate, to help with some of the more difficult decisions. This is also a good "Mother-Daughter" task. Remember to weed out your old stockings, socks, undies, bathing suits, gym clothes and belts.

Re-hang your clothes in an organized fashion according to a plan. Some plans might be:

Pants by color, Tops by color, Sweaters by color, Coats, Dresses and Dressy outfits or Sweatpants, Jeans, Dress pants, T-shirts, Blouses, Sweaters, Skirts, Dresses, Suits.

As you begin wearing clothes out of your newly-organized closet, you will realize that those purple pants do not have a top to go with them. This is when you begin phase two of the organized closet. Phase two is your shopping list. Keep a list in your purse of needed clothing items. (You can even list what you are willing to spend on each item.) London prefers to write her list on a dry-erase board in her room. When you have saved up the funds, or the time to go shopping, bring your list and complete your wardrobe. Have fun! Bring a friend along to aid in the "search."

Include a dirty clothes hamper in your closet, and use it. Mom believes in the golden rule of no clothes on the floor, chair, or counter, ever, unless you're sick. London prefers the "pile" approach; new clothes in a pile, dirty clothes in another pile in the hamper, and planned outfits in a third pile. Sometimes she even begins a fourth pile which would be entitled, "I thought this was cute to wear, but then I changed my mind. I'll hang it back up soon."

Accessories are your friends. Keep them in order. Belts and scarves should be rolled in a drawer or hung on hooks. Jewelry needs to be in a cabinet or jewelry box, and sorted into color sections or sections by type, i.e., ear-rings, bracelets, necklaces, etc. Purses can be lined up on a shelf or hung on hooks. Hats are best in hat boxes (tape a photo of the hat(s) on the outside of the hat box so you know what's inside.) If you wear a lot of baseball caps, remember to periodically take them with you into the shower and give them a good scrubbing.

Shoes must be comfortable. If your feet hurt, you will not have fun. My friend, Mimi Casey, always says, "If I see a woman in a bad mood, chances are her feet hurt!" The best time to shop for shoes is in the afternoon after a long day of walking. Look for shoes that are attractive, in a color that matches your clothing, and that have versatility. Then organize your shoes according to season. During the summer, move your sandals to the front of the shoe rack or shelf. Boots can take a back seat. Then, when autumn rolls around, shift those sandals to the rear. Remember, it is often better to repair or polish a favorite pair of shoes than to replace them.

Watches keep you on time. Enjoy them. Twice a year (when we change the clocks) I take all of my watches in to get new batteries. This way, I do not have to run to the store in a panic when my watch batteries run out. Some teens prefer checking their cell phones for the time. Always keep a cell phone charger in your car.

CHAPTER 4

SHARING A BATHROOM
WITH A BROTHER
OR MATE

In an ideal world, we might all have our own bathrooms, but if you need to share one here are some tips.

1. The theme of "Divide and Conquer Clutter" will set the stage for a fun bathroom experience. When sharing a bathroom, it is necessary to divide up the available counter and drawer space. Once you know which drawers belong to you, you can begin organizing them.

2. Designate one drawer for makeup. Use a plastic silverware divider, or small boxes without lids to separate your makeup into blushes, lipsticks, eye shadows, etc. You can use a pretty mug on the counter for your brushes and pencils. Just be sure to keep the utensils to a minimum, and toss old ones. Our rule of thumb is, "If you haven't used it in a year, it's time to toss it."

3. Another drawer should be devoted to skin care. Include your soap, sun screen, moisturizer, acne lotions, and any other creams and concoctions.

4. If you have room, use a third drawer for tools. This should include tweezers, scissors, nail polish, blow dryers, curling irons, curlers and flat irons.

5. Use your bathroom cabinet for tampons, pads, hair products, and extra supplies. Just like in your office, keep one extra bottle of each skin care product, make up, and necessary items "on hold" for when you run out. Replace the extra bottle a.s.a.p. once you use begin using it, or

store the empty in your "replenishment box" (a box to keep empties that need to be replaced next time you go shopping.)

6. Cleaning the toilet and emptying out the trash are the hardest areas to negotiate with a brother/mate. We can only suggest that you divide these two chores up by each selecting one and sticking to your promise to do it. Promising to do it means that you and your brother/mate should never notice that the trash can is overflowing, and that the toilet is yucky. Rotate jobs annually if at all.

7. Your medicine cabinet is for medicine and can be shared with your brother/mate. Keep your prescription drugs in the original containers and get new prescriptions filled before you run out. Keep organized by having common medicines available at all times in your cabinet.

Medicine Cabinet Basics:
- pain killers (Tylenol, Advil, etc.)
- band aids
- cough syrup
- decongestant
- antacid
- anti-bacterial lotion, i.e. Neosporin
- a thermometer
- rubbing alcohol or hydrogen peroxide

Make sure your brother/mate knows that when something is running low, it is time to replace it.

CHAPTER 5

YOUR HOMEWORK, LOCKER AND FREE TIME

How could we lump together a teenager's least favorite (homework) and most favorite (free time) words into the same chapter? Because being organized with homework leads to more free time and more fun.

Begin by setting up an assignment book. (See our sample page.) Fill in your daily, weekly, and long term assignments as they are assigned. It is important to include the due date and daily work as well. Highlight tests, quizzes, and due dates of projects. If you prefer to keep track of assignments and appointments in a computerized calendar, i.e. a blackberry, keep it charged and updated nightly.

Your locker is your "room away from home." Instead of just a place to throw books, make it your organizational pit-stop. Keep a box inside with extra pens and pencils, some protein bars, a bottle of water, your hairbrush, tampons, sunscreen, lip gloss, a mirror, and any other supplies you think you may need. I like to keep an extra sweater or jacket in my locker in case the weather turns cold. I use locker shelves and a hanging bag with pockets to maximize my use of the locker space available.

The key to having more free time is in "structuring" your time. This means that you keep a list of phone calls you need to return, and you return them all at one sitting. You check and return email all at one sitting. Schedule your chores, errands, workouts, and practice times so that you know when you will have free time. When your free time arrives, don't answer the phone, don't check your mail, just enjoy your uninterrupted time all to yourself. This free time will revitalize you and give you more energy to complete tasks afterwards. Schedule at least fifteen minutes of free time everyday. As you begin to organize yourself, you will find this amount of free time steadily increases.

Sample Assignment book   Week of_____

Classes:	Monday	Tuesday	Wednesday	Thursday	Friday
Period 1					
Period 2					
Period 3					
Period 4					
Period 5					
Period 6					
Period 7					
Period 8					
After School					

Write your classes down the left side of the table. Write the assignments in the spaces which list the dates they are due. If using a computerized calendar, keep a printout of your monthly assignments posted above your desk. For mothers of younger children or mothers who have care-takers at home, a copy of the computerized schedule can be hung on the refrigerator or bulletin board so all family members know the daily plans.

CHAPTER 6

SETTLING ARGUMENTS

Arguments are a natural part of human to human communication. The goal of an argument is not to get your way, but instead to reach a compromise that both individuals are comfortable with. Think of it not as an argument, but as a negotiation.

During a negotiation, it is easier to think of a clever compromise if your emotions are kept at bay. If you find yourself screaming, crying, or becoming silent … postpone the negotiation for a few hours. (I enjoy listening to some of my favorite music during this "cool down" time to re-set my mood.)

Sibling arguments occur daily. Some basic rules, however, are required to keep the arguments civilized. In our home, we have all agreed that there will be no physical element to the arguments, and there will be no name-calling. Additionally, arguments should be "private" and not held in front of friends.

As a parent, it is important to identify subjects that cause the same arguments repeatedly. Making a family policy regarding that subject will help eliminate future arguments. In our home, the kids often argued about who got to sit in the front seat of the car. One child would try to yell, "Dibbs on the front seat!" London, the eldest, would try to use the argument that her legs were longer, so she deserved the front seat at all times. As parents, my husband and I settled the arguing by setting a new family policy. London would get the front seat of the "even" dates of the month, and her brother would get it on the "odd" dates. We haven't had a "seat argument" since. Some common sibling arguments topics include family chores, control of the TV. tuner, use of the family computer, and portion size of food. All of these can be solved by devising new family policies.

Family policies can also solve arguments between spouses. My husband and I found that we continually argued over two subjects; what to watch on TV. and at what temperature should we set the home thermostat. We decided on a new policy that has worked for us for twenty-three years. I control the TV.

at all times, and he controls the thermostat at all times. We both are delighted with this arrangement. Friends of ours sometimes laugh at our other "family policies," but they work for us in keeping arguments to a minimum. For years, I was upset when my husband came home late from work, and my home-cooked delicious dinner was "ruined." Those arguments were a thing of the past once we instituted a new policy; my husband pays me $1.00 for every minute he is late for dinner on the first late day of the week. If he is late a second day that same week, the rate goes up to $2.00 per minute, and so on. One of our crazier policies states that my husband never has to empty the dishwasher, and I never have to carry my purse when he is with me.

We found that the easiest way to negotiate a family policy is through writing. Writing your ideas and solutions down on paper helps to remove the emotional context that can get in the way during an "in person" argument. Here are the steps:

1. Begin your negotiation with either both or one individual writing down what is bothering them, along with three possible solutions. Do not discuss the issue verbally.

2. Trade papers.

3. Write out a response to the listed solutions, and try to avoid harsh, accusatory statements.

4. Trade papers.

5. Continue this trading process until a compromise is reached.

When negotiating with your teenager, I have found that avoiding "verbal discussion" during a negotiation is the key to remaining calm and reaching an agreeable solution. An interesting note is that the "trading process" can occur over a series of days. Some arguments take time to reach a solution. Be patient, exchange notes once each day, and keep the process going.

Family rules are needed in order for parents and teens to keep the arguments down to a minimum. We have found that three family rules are sufficient for keeping the peace.

1. Be respectful

2. Do what's safe

3. Always keep in touch

If you think of common teen problem areas, i.e. parties, driving, chores, friends, school work, etc. you can see how easily these three rules apply to most everything. Keep them posted around your home and refer to them often. When one of the three rules is broken, we prefer to brainstorm answers as to what would have been a better action than the one that was taken. This doesn't mean that a consequence isn't in order; it simply takes care of organizing a better plan for the future. I believe that our job as parents is to prepare our children to be successful adults in the real world. I've found that following these three rules seem to serve you well in all endeavors.

CHAPTER 7

HOUSEHOLD CHORES

Household chores will continue until you are dead. That being said, they can be done in an organized fashion so that you can continue to have time for fun. To begin with, every member who lives in the house must have assigned chores. To begin the process, make a list of everything that needs to be done. We keep our list divided into three sections:

1. Weekly Chores

2. Monthly Chores

3. Long-term Chores

The intriguing aspect about most families is that certain people gravitate toward certain chores. In our home, Mom likes shopping for food, doing the dishes, and folding laundry. Dad enjoys cooking meals, hiring subcontractors, and washing the car. Fourteen-Year-Old Hunter enjoys doing the dishes, collecting trash, and making dessert. London prefers baking and setting the table. Once you have developed your list of chores, set up a chore chart with a list of family member's names next to the chores they prefer.

What about the "yucky" chores that nobody wants? The doggie-duty-pick up? The toilet bowl cleaning? Lump these jobs into groups, and rotate responsibility for them on a weekly basis. If your children fall into many age groups, you can separate the chores by difficulty level. For example, when I was a child, each family member was required to cook breakfast one day per week. The eldest (me) had to make omelets, bacon, potatoes, and orange juice on my day. The youngest (my sister) got out the cereal boxes and milk on her day each week.

What about chores that aren't carried out? A simple reminder should be tried first. If the reminder falls on deaf ears, it may be time to institute some of the monthly chores or long-term chores, performed under supervision. For example, a child who neglects to do the dinner dishes after a "kind" reminder may be asked to polish the silver the following afternoon.

<u>Chore chart</u>

Name_____Week of _____

Date	6AM to 8 AM	8AM to 3PM	3PM to 5PM	5PM to 7PM	7PM to 10PM	Break-fast dishes	Set table Clear table Break-fast	Set table Clear table lunch	Lunch dishes	Set table Clear table Dinner	Dinner dishes	Practice Musical instru-ment 15 min. daily
Mon												
Tues												
Wed												
Thur												
Fri												

Weekly Jobs: Make bed, Clean room, Brush teeth twice, Put away clothes

Special assignments_____

Circle Additional Jobs As Needed:

Walk the dog	Weed the yard	Moe the grass	Clean the windows	Clean the _____
Wash the car	Wash clothes	Iron:	Cook:	Help with _____
Baby-sit:	Drive:	Polish:	Put away:	Do:

CHAPTER 8

ENTERTAINING

If you are reading this section, then you are not a Martha Stewart type who has a passion for hostessing. Anyone can become an organized hostess and enjoy entertaining, it just takes a few simple steps and a little bit of practice. Ask yourself what you have enjoyed at other parties. What made that particular party memorable and fun? Sometimes it's the dynamic make-up of the guest list, sometimes it's the entertainment or food, and sometimes it's an activity held during the party. Try to duplicate any concepts that "strike a cord" with you. Begin by asking yourself the following questions:

1. Who would you like to entertain? Friends? Business associates/clients? Extended family? Begin by coming up with a number and a list of potential guests.

2. Once you have your guest number, can you seat them at tables in your home or will the party be less formal?

3. Do you want to cook, purchase or cater?

4. What time of day or evening would you like to entertain?

5. What is your budget?

Once you have answered the above questions, you are ready to begin. Make a guest list and invite your guests. (Use phone, email, or paper invitations.) Include an R.S.V.P. date. If you will be cooking, select recipes that you enjoy making. Make a grocery list and timeline. If you will be purchasing the food, place an order and select a time to pick it up. If catering is your plan, call friends for references and select a caterer. They will direct you from that point on.

One week before the party, check your supplies. Do you have enough plates, glasses, silverware? Do you have decorations, table cloths, and music? Have all of your RSVPs come in? Leave you calendar open that week to track down any necessary items. Will you be arranging specific seating? Will you provide name

Everyone brought beach chairs and blankets. We passed around pop-corn and candy bars.)

5. If using a disc jockey, discuss the types or songs you want him to play and whether or not you want him to host dance games/contests. Make sure you have purchased prizes if you plan contests.

6. If the party is a birthday celebration, provide an empty table where guests can place their gifts.

7. Keep the party area separate from the rest of your home. I held my party in the yard and garage and just allowed access to one indoor bathroom. I made signs on the other doors that said "No Admittance."

8. Hire a few "bodyguards" to keep everyone in line, or ask your parents and their friends to "circulate" every 15–20 minutes.

9. Be sure to clean up the mess the next day, and get your friends to help. That way your parents will let you have another party!

<u>Teen Party Rules</u>

✓ No leaving the home yard fenced area (to walk the streets or go to cars)

✓ No admittance to home. Use bathroom by pool

✓ Out-of-control behavior will mean immediate removal from the party via taxi or parents.

✓ Departure no later than 11:00 PM

✓ Have fun, be safe, and make good decisions!

CHAPTER 9

VACATIONS

Taking a vacation is intended to be a nice break from your everyday life. Some vacations are for gaining knowledge and visiting sights. Other trips are for relaxation or to spend time as a "family" or as a "couple." Whatever the intent of the trip, the preliminary planning and organization is what will allow you to have fun! Take the time to set up your trip, and you will be rewarded when you travel.

Begin by selecting your destination. Some families like the tradition of vacationing in the same locale year after year. Others enjoy the hunt to find a new enticing spot. My brother, Todd, enjoys adventure vacations that involve strenuous activities such as climbing Mount Kilimanjaro. He and his family enjoy the preparation and training involved months before the actual vacation begins. Start with a family meeting and write down suggested vacation spots or types of vacations desired. Assign a little research to each family member, and then hold a second meeting about a week later. Once the suggestions are on the table, it's time to narrow down the list by taking into consideration price, dates, availability, and preferences. It may be necessary to select a certain vacation for the current year, and the promise of a different type of vacation the following year. Keep your notes in a vacation folder.

Once a destination and date have been selected, the trip planning really begins. I prefer to use my "Trip Plan Check List" to make sure all the details have been organized. Everyone remembers to book their flights and hotel accommodations, but there are many other details to plan as well. Remember to select seat assignments, set up rides to and from your destination, book restaurant reservations, excursions, and activities (i.e. golf, spa, lessons, etc.) Purchasing a guide book can help in selecting your best options for all of the above. In addition, talk to friends who may have traveled to the same location. "Insider tips" are invaluable. A simple email to friends notifying them of your vacation destination can bring back a wealth of knowledge.

Trip Plan Check List

Trip to:_____

Dates:_____

- ❑ Airline Tickets_____
- ❑ Seat assignments_____
- ❑ Boarding Passes
- ❑ Ride to Airport
- ❑ Airport Requirements:_____
- ❑ Ride from destination to hotel
- ❑ Ride back to Airport from hotel
- ❑ Ride from Airport to home
- ❑ Rental Car_____
- ❑ Hotel Reservations_____
- ❑ Market List_____
- ❑ Dinner Reservations_____
  _____
  _____
- ❑ Excursions_____
  _____
  _____
- ❑ Spa Appointments_____
- ❑ Golf Tee Times_____
- ❑ Travel Book, etc … _____

One week before your trip is the time to cancel any mail or newspaper deliveries, notify trusted neighbors, and begin your packing process. Adults and teens can pack for themselves using the "Packing List." Younger children can also pack for themselves if you list quantity numbers on the lines next to each item, or circle necessities.

Packing List

- ❑ Pajamas_____
- ❑ Underwear/long underwear/bras/slips_____
- ❑ Shoes: ___tennis shoes, ___dress shoes, ____boots___Sandals/flip flops
- ❑ Pants: _____casual _____dressy
- ❑ Shorts: _____
- ❑ Shirts: _____t-shirt _____collared
- ❑ Bathing suits_____
- ❑ Work-out clothes: _____
- ❑ Skirts_____
- ❑ Dresses: _____ casual _____dressy
- ❑ Socks_____
- ❑ Sweaters_____ pashminas_____
- ❑ Coats _____
- ❑ Jackets: casual_____ suit_____
- ❑ Hats: _____for shade _____for warmth
- ❑ Toothbrush/toothpaste
- ❑ Hairbrush, Hair dryer, flat iron
- ❑ facial soap(s) and make up
- ❑ Sunscreen, Bug repellant, Aloe
- ❑ Books and Magazines
- ❑ Games and Electronics: cell phone, computer, DVD's, CD's, i-Pod, head-phones, speakers, chargers, playing cards, family board games,
- ❑ Sports Equipment: skateboards, surfboards, golf club, snorkel gear, boogie boards,
- ❑ Ties: _____ Belts: _____
- ❑ Jewelry: _____Gloves and scarves: _____
- ❑ Purses, backpacks, umbrellas, wallet: _____
- ❑ Pillow for airplane/bed: _____
- ❑ Medicines, contact lens, vitamins: _____

- ❏ Food: cereal, tea, snacks: _____
- ❏ Eye glasses/sun glasses: _____
- ❏ Airplane tickets/Boarding passes/lounge admittance card: _____
- ❏ Travel guide _____

Chapter 10

Exercise

I used to think that the result of exercise was exhaustion. Mom explained to me that after you exercise, you actually have more energy. If you have more energy, you can have more fun! So, exercise is an important part of being organized. The good part about it is that there are so many types to choose from. The key is to find the one that you like, so you can stick with it.

Begin by thinking about what you like to do in your spare time. If you like to listen to music, then walking with earphones and music is a good bet. If you prefer to read in your spare time, then get a book on tape to listen to while exercising. They also have lectures and television shows that you can download onto an i-Pod. If dancing is your favorite activity, then take a dance class or dance to a video at home. Some friends we know prefer competitive sports. There are all sorts of leagues and clubs available where you can challenge others while exercising. Some of Mom's friends need "time to talk with girlfriends" so they set up weekly walks throughout the neighborhood and they chat away while walking. My Dad; he prefers working with a personal trainer on the beach. If you put you mind to it; you should be able to come up with a weekly activity that you enjoy, and that also involves exercise. You'll be glad you did.

Once you have an idea for an enjoyable exercise activity, ask yourself if the activity meets your exercise and medical goals. If you are seeking a healthy heart you will most likely need a different activity than if you are seeking to be more flexible. Ask yourself if you are exercising to lose weight, release stress, relax, or increase endurance. If your chosen activity doesn't mesh well with your exercise goals, you will need to supplement it with another activity, or make a few alterations to the chosen exercise. I enjoy Pilates for the strength and flexibility it provides, however, I must supplement my workouts with bi-weekly walks in the hills to promote heart health and endurance. I really don't enjoy the walks very much, but I listen to books on tape while I walk, and that helps pass the time.

Reward yourself after completion of a consistent exercise program. We both like to go out and buy a new exercise outfit as a special reward. Find a reward that motivates you and keeps you on track. If you are working out with a buddy, you can give each other gifts as your rewards, or celebrate with a meal at a special restaurant.

To stay organized with your exercise plan, you have to list your exercise "appointments" into your schedule. Make them as important as your hairdresser appointments, and don't cancel them. A good motivational rule to follow is: when you cancel an exercise appointment, you must reschedule it with two more.

CHAPTER 11

TWENTY-THREE THINGS YOU NEED TO KNOW BEFORE YOU LEAVE HOME

Mom and I came up with this list when we started to think about colleges and my moving out. It freaked me out when Mom said that she was running out of time to teach me everything I needed to know before I left home. I told her that she could always teach me, even when I'm gone, and I could always ask her for help. We thought coming up with a list was a good way to begin to see what was involved, and I discovered that I'm well on my way!

<u>The Twenty-three Things</u>
1. How to write a check and balance a checking account
2. How to do laundry
3. How to shop for and prepare a breakfast, lunch, and dinner
4. How to find a doctor
5. How to set up and work with a budget
6. How to set up and use an electronic or paper address book
7. How to calculate a tip in a restaurant
8. How to keep track of important dates and appointments
9. How to pick a mate
10. How to tell when you need medical care
11. How to drive a car

12. How to find a place to live and arrange for internet, telephone and cable TV service

13. How to get out of a building in case of fire

14. How to act appropriately when someone you know dies

15. How and when to write a thank you note

16. How to book a flight and a hotel for a trip

17. How to dress for social situations that are labeled "casual," "business casual," "cocktail attire," "semi-formal," "formal," and "black tie."

18. How to exercise

19. How to relieve stress

20. How to address an envelope, assemble and mail a package, and write a formal letter

21. How to give back to society through community service

22. How to express and develop your spiritual side

23. How to examine your failures and turn them into learning experiences so that you can grow stronger

CHAPTER 12

RELAXATION

This chapter is our shortest because it's the most simple. Relaxation can be broken down into three distinct areas:

1. Making time to relax
2. Learning how to relax
3. Convincing yourself that relaxing is good, necessary, and a priority.

Let's begin with the first one, making time to relax means finding a few spare minutes in your day. That's possible for everyone. Two minutes of relaxation can revitalize you for hours afterwards. Look at it like "going to the bathroom." No matter how busy your day is, you must take time to go to the bathroom. The same applies for relaxation.

Learning how to relax can take some practice. Don't give up. Begin by closing your eyes, tensing your muscles, and then releasing your muscles. Do muscle groups together, i.e. legs, face, arms, feet, etc … Slow down your breathing to an inhale for three seconds and an exhale for three seconds. Breathe in and out through your nose, and try to use your diaphragm to get air, not just your lungs. Do this for two to five minutes, twice a day, or as often as needed. That's it. You've just accomplished relaxing. If you notice during the day that your breathing is speeding up, that's a signal that it's time to relax.

Don't we all agree that relaxing is good? If you look at the opposite statement, "relaxing is bad," we all accept that as being false. Everyone deserves to relax. Everyone deserves to be around others who have taken the time to relax each day. This applies to parents, spouses, and kids! It's what makes the world a more peaceful spot. If you still have trouble prioritizing your relaxing, tell yourself it's your way of contributing to world peace!

Some easy places to try the "relaxed breathing" are:

- While in traffic
- While in line
- While listening to someone who is making you feel stressed
- Before a task that makes you feel nervous, i.e., a final exam
- When you're late for an appointment
- When you have to make an uncomfortable phone call
- When you've disappointed someone
- When you want to think of a good idea or be creative

CHAPTER 13

Now That You're Organized, How to Have Fun!

Begin by making a list of what you thought was fun when you were a kid. Here's Mom's list:

- Tap dancing
- Coloring
- Swinging on the monkey bars
- Playing board games
- Eating chocolate pudding
- Listening to a record (no C.D.'s then) and reading/singing the lyrics along with the song
- Taking walks along the rocks at the beach
- Making macramé necklaces
- Painting rocks to make door jams
- Sewing clothes for school dances
- Doing needlepoint and knitting

Just doing this list brought a smile to Mom's face. Next add to your list any activities that you've discovered you enjoy lately.

- Oil painting
- Pilates
- Photoshop
- Teaching others

<u>Recipe for having fun:</u>

Select from your list above one activity to do per week. Schedule it into your calendar. Once you've accomplished this, try to fit in two activities per week, and so on. Some activities may be long term, so keep them going. Others may be a once a year thing (sewing an outfit) but fun while you do it. Aim for one fun activity per day.

Keep an open mind. Continuously seek to discover new activities that bring fun into your life. If you find yourself thinking, "That was really fun," do it again soon! Find friends that share your idea of fun. And finally, help them to get organized, so they can have fun!

THE BONUS WORDS
OF WISDOM
CHAPTERS

CHAPTER 14

FINDING A COLLEGE

We weren't going to add this section to the book, but then we thought about how much easier and more fun this process is now that we have our "College Critique" and "College Application" charts. So, when visiting and applying to colleges, use these handy charts to keep track of what you think of the school, and when your application materials are due.

College Critique Chart

Name of College	Liked	Disliked	Issues	Further Questions

The best procedure requires applying to ten different colleges. Select three schools that would be considered a "reach" for you to get into. Select four schools that are in your "zone." Lastly, select three schools that are "safety" schools where it's quite certain that you would be accepted. Your school counselor or a college guidebook can help you decide which categories particular schools fall into for you based on your grade point average and your S.A.T. or A.C.T. scores.

College Application Chart

Name of College	SAT Reasoning Scores reported, due by	SAT Subject Scores reported, due by	Early Decision deadline	College will notify student of Early Decision by	Early Action deadline	College will notify student of Early Action by	Regular Application deadline	Priority Application deadline	Rolling application deadline	Set up interview with admission by	Interview date/time	College will notify student by	Student must reply to acceptance by

Chapter 15

Getting Organized to Pick a Boyfriend/Mate

The most important decision you will ever make is not your career, your place of residency, or your choice of friends. It is who you choose as your mate for life! Such an important decision requires several skills such as self-knowledge, research, and interviewing techniques. These skills are often neglected in school classes and in childrearing lectures from our parents. The only way to learn them is to acknowledge their necessity, and to practice them. Through practice, success will be achieved, and you will pick the right boyfriend/mate for you.

Self-Knowledge is the first skill utilized in picking a mate. You must first know yourself. Are you a talker or a listener? A party person or a privacy seeker? Ambitious? Competitive? A big spender? Do you get along better with someone who agrees with you? When in an argument do you fight or flee? Begin by spending some time thinking about your past friendships. Make a list of the attributes in your good friends. Make a list of the characteristics in friends that bother you or cause you not to get along well with them. Examine your lists and come up with traits to look for and traits to avoid in a potential mate. Here's a sample:

> I am looking for a mate who is: Trustworthy, a good listener, compassionate, athletic, social, likes music, cares about his family, is intelligent, and ambitious.

> I will avoid a mate who is: Bossy, too talkative, very private, sedentary, aggressive, and likes to tease.

Attributes for my mate
My current good friends have the following attributes:
1.
2.
3.
4.
5.
6.
7.
8.
9.
10.
11.
12.
13.
14.

People that bother me have the following attributes:
1.
2.
3.
4.
5.

My mate **MUST** have the following characteristics: (religious preference, hobbies, interests, goals, residency in a certain part of the world, desire to have a family, personality, looks, etc …)
1.
2.
3.
4.
5.

My mate **MUST NOT** have the following characteristics:
1.
2.
3.
4.
5.

Once you have your list compiled, you are ready to begin the research part of the process. Unlike researching a term paper, your research for a mate typically does not involve internet sources or books. Your research involves asking yourself this one question:

Where would my potential mate "hang out?" If your list of attributes includes someone who is athletic; a gym, playing field, or bike path would be a good spot to look. Searching for a music-lover might be done in a music store, at a concert, or in a live-music club. Some of the research requires deeper thought. Where would a compassionate person hang out? (Charity events, Special Olympics, Big Brother Organization.) Where would an ambitious person be found? (Business seminars, Young Executives meetings, a weekday lunch restaurant that caters to nearby offices.) If you are stumped, ask friends. They can be a great resource. Once you have researched your locations, then go to them! Look around you, as you are ready to begin the last step, the interview process.

When you see a mate that "strikes your fancy," you are ready to begin the interview process. Smile and strike up a conversation. This does not mean that you run through a list of questions as if you were performing a job interview. It means, that you carry on a normal conversation, but you make a "mental note" of your potential mate's answers that may or may not reflect the characteristics in question. As you begin dating, note during your conversations, does he mention working out? Does he talk a lot or listen to you? Does he seem intelligent? Polite? If family is important to you, try mentioning your family and see how he reacts. Discuss your passions and goals and compare them with his.

The interview process can be as long or as short as it takes for you to decide whether or not the potential mate has the characteristics you are seeking. Once you are sure that he does not have those characteristics, move on! Do not waste time with someone who doesn't have the potential you are looking for. Go back to research and start over.

Once you have determined that this person has the characteristics you are seeking, you can refine your interview process with direct questions. This is best done while on a "date." Make sure you discuss childrearing, religion, spending money, sex, in-laws, work, and home life before you get married. It's always a good idea to discuss anything controversial before you take the big leap. When your mate truly knows the real you and you truly know him then you can be sure you have found the right person. My friend, Randy Fifield, says "If you have been dating for three months and you are still unsure, that's a sign to move on."

A personal note on dating; dating is practice in finding a lifetime mate. Despite what many teenagers think, it is not just about hanging out, hooking up, or having fun. Dating allows you to learn more about yourself, how you interact with a mate, and what kind of mate gets along best with you. The same advice applies during the interview process. Once you know the boyfriend is not for you, move on! If the boyfriend breaks up with you, consider it an easy way to move into the research stage since he clearly wasn't the right mate for you. Finding a mate is not a contest to be won, but a match to be made.

My Dad, London's Grandfather, gave me a list on my 16th birthday of 107 attributes that he felt I should seek in a potential mate. I remember reading over the list, laughing, and thinking that it would be impossible. I promptly put the list away in a drawer. When I had my first date later that year, I remember thinking about the list for a fleeting moment. Eight years later, I re-read the list and realized that many of the items weren't important to me at all, and were in fact just my Dad's vision of a mate. Other items, however, had become "deal breakers." When I set out to find my potential mate, I had my personal list hidden in the back of my mind. After speaking with my "future" husband for three hours on Saint Patrick's Day, I knew he was the one!

Our family comes from a tradition of embracing organization. London's Grandfather and Grandmother were engaged one month after dating, and got married two months later. They celebrated their fiftieth anniversary this year. My husband and I got engaged after five months (although I knew he was the one the evening we met) and were married eight months later. We celebrated our twenty-third anniversary this year. The pattern is prevalent throughout our extended family. Being organized has lead to lifelong marriage success.

Seventy-eight-Year-Old Grandfather Barry Miller's List of Attributes
to Seek in a Mate

1.   Good health habits
2.   Soft pleasant voice
3.   Best possible appearance—good posture
4.   Speaks without grammatical errors
5.   Optimistic—doesn't put others down
6.   Not sarcastic
7.   Enthusiastic
8.   Appreciative
9.   Smiles easily
10. Pleasant to be with—cheerful—joyful
11. Makes others around you feel comfortable
12. Interested in others—excited to meet new people
13. Discusses proper subject matter in conversation (nothing too personal)
14. Thinks positively
15. Spouse and family comes first (basic theory only)
16. Helpful—quick to volunteer
17. Humble
18. Respectful
19. On time
20. Clean minded
21. Aware and in-tune intuitively with people and surroundings
22. Courteous—Gentlemanly/ladylike, good manners
23. Lots of interests
24. Doesn't exaggerate
25. Reliable
26. Success in his or her chosen field
27. Considerate
28. Trustworthy
29. Intelligent

30. Current and in-style

31. Keeps one's word

32. Loyal

33. Sincere

34. Gives honest compliments to others

35. Honest—Truthful

36. Not a braggart—Modest

37. Practices moderation

38. Knows when to and when not to give advice

39. Under control—has self discipline

40. Not pushy

41. Not rude

42. Conforms to certain conventions

43. Shows consideration of others' feelings—thoughtful

44. No temper (or control of it)

45. Not a complainer

46. Able to take charge—shows responsibility

47. Knowledgeable

48. Warm

49. Alert

50. Can deal with problems—problem solver (not creator)

51. Calm

52. Can express oneself clearly

53. Up on basic current events, music, sports, etc.

54. Mature

55. Hard working

56. Fits into various groups

57. Good listener

58. Ambitious

59. Sense of humor

60. Even-tempered disposition

61. Can keep a secret
62. Thanks people
63. Demonstrates the 10 Commandments—devotion—reverence
64. Nice
65. Believes in oneself
66. Not judgmental
67. Does one's best—not afraid to give it your all
68. Doesn't give up—keeps trying—perseverance—steadfastness
69. Demonstrates commitment
70. Has confidence
71. Creative
72. Determined
73. Demonstrates excellence
74. Shows forgiveness
75. Generous
76. Honorable
77. Takes initiative
78. Has integrity
79. Can love
80. Patient
81. Peaceful
82. Purposeful
83. Can sacrifice when necessary
84. Wise
85. Has zeal
86. Charitable
87. Adventurous
88. Flexible
89. Hospitable
90. Not afraid to try new things
91. Mentally and physically fit

92. Informed
93. Makes eye contact with others
94. Remembers names and uses them in conversation
95. Has a non-victim mentality
96. For women—nurturing
97. Well-read in classics
98. Proud
99. Patriotic
100. Cooperative
101. Bilingual
102. Votes and participates in civic duties
103. Tolerant
104. Just
105. Tactful
106. Courageous
107. Understands life's three great teachers: Experience, Observation, and Reasoning

Life is in the journey, so enjoy each step on your path. Organize yourself and you will have more time for additional fun along the way.

978-0-595-45072-5
0-595-45072-5

CPSIA information can be obtained
at www.ICGtesting.com
Printed in the USA
LVHW030139301120
672984LV00054B/1502